Real Estate Management

Table of Contents

Introduction

Chapter 1: Flipping

Chapter 2: Investing in Purchases

Chapter 3: Investing in Rentals

Chapter 4: Investing in Financial Transactions

Chapter 5: Representing

Chapter 6: Developing

Chapter 7: Diversifying

Chapter 8: Bonus Money Making Ideas

Conclusion

© Copyright 2018 by __DavidClement___ - All rights reserved.

The following eBook is reproduced below with the goal of providing information that is as accurate and reliable as possible. Regardless, purchasing this eBook can be seen as consent to the fact that both the publisher and the author of this book are in no way experts on the topics discussed within and that any recommendations or suggestions that are made herein are for entertainment purposes only. Professionals should be consulted as needed prior to undertaking any of the action endorsed herein.

This declaration is deemed fair and valid by both the American Bar Association and the Committee of Publishers Association and is legally binding throughout the United States.

Furthermore, the transmission, duplication, or reproduction of any of the following work including specific information will be considered an illegal act irrespective of whether it is done electronically or in print. This extends to creating a secondary or tertiary copy of the work or a recorded copy and is only allowed with an expressed written consent from the Publisher. All additional rights reserved.

The information in the following pages is broadly considered to be a truthful and accurate account of facts and as such any inattention, use or misuse of the information in question by the reader will render any resulting actions solely under their purview. There are no scenarios in which the publisher or the original author of this work can be, in any fashion, deemed liable for any hardship or damages that may befall them after undertaking information described herein.

Additionally, the information in the following pages is intended only for informational purposes and should thus be thought of as universal. As befitting its nature, it is presented without assurance regarding its prolonged validity or interim quality. Trademarks are mentioned without written consent and can in no way be considered an endorsement from the trademark holder.

Introduction

Congratulations on downloading *Retail Estate Management* and thank you for doing so.

The following chapters will discuss different methods for generating revenue through various real estate tactics. Some of the concepts introduced in this book may be obvious income generators and things you have already thought of while others may be new concepts that you had no idea even existed. Even the concepts that you already know about which are discussed here will hopefully provide ideas and explanations that will help you in your pursuit of becoming an incredibly successful real estate professional.

As you begin on this career venture, there are some choices you need to make which will set a foundation for yourself so you can start raking in money. Many of which are highlighted throughout this book. If you are a savvy professional who wants to get even more out of your industry, there are plenty of suggestions in here for you too. And for everyone in between, there are many ideas and avenues for making money with real estate. Thankfully, this industry is vast and diverse which allows you to pick and choose a path to success that works with your values and desires. Be smart, choose wisely, and you can reap big rewards!

There are plenty of books on this subject on the market, so thanks again for choosing this one! Every effort was made to ensure it is full of as much useful information as possible, please enjoy!

Chapter 1: Flipping

If you are looking for an amazing short-term strategy for making money with real estate, 'flipping' homes is an excellent option. The basic concept is to find an undervalued home that would benefit from renovations, complete the necessary renovations and then sell the home for a profit. If you have watched any HGTV, then most likely you have seen this process in action. It is important to keep in mind that this process of fixing and flipping is not as easy as it may appear.

Another option is to flip contracts rather than fixing up and flipping a home. In this chapter, both concepts will be outlined for you to discover the moneymaking potential of both.

One of the biggest problems people face when they are looking at fixing and flipping homes is the misconception that you do not have to get your hands dirty. This takes a lot of hard work, and that automatically includes exhausting manual labor. This real estate moneymaker is one of the most practical and profitable options available, and you may find that it's worth the effort.

But how exactly do you successfully flip a house or a contract? One of the most important preliminary steps is to understand the market around you. You are looking for a seller that needs to get out of their house fast. You also want to get an idea of what your buyers would be like. The ideal buyer is one who is willing and able to pay cash. The reason you why you need to look into this is so that you can find, renovate, and sell a house or negotiate a transaction in as little time as possible. Knowing how many people need to sell, who can buy, and in what areas these people are most commonly located can help you become more successful.

If you are not already connected with buyers who can pay cash, there are a few other methods you can use. Marketing online and running ads targeted at cash buyers is one such method. Consider advertising on Facebook or even offering a webinar. Another method is to use the data from county records. This will require time and effort, but there is an amazing amount of information available just waiting to be discovered which makes it worth the hard work. When you comb through these records, you can find all the county's transactions that were cash and who the buyers were. It also includes contact information!

Once you have interested and available buyers, it is time to locate your sellers and get ready to flip. Once you have a seller, you can choose to purchase the home yourself and renovate it before selling it to your buyers, or you can be the link between the seller and the buyer before anything is done to the home.

Fixing and flipping houses requires you to buy a house, fix it up, and sell it for a profit. This process does require a large initial investment and carries a large risk. It is possible for you to lose money trying to resell a home you already purchased. To be successful at fixing and flipping houses, you consider the following tips:

- Choose a house in a good neighborhood, in decent condition, in a good school zone, and listed below market value. It is important that the house only requires fixes like painting, flooring or lighting. Quick updates to the kitchen are easy and impactful. If a house requires more costly renovations like a new roof, mold treatment, or electrical rewiring you may want to consider the investment versus the potential income potential and the time involved in the repairs. Also, the kitchen especially should be in good condition or require only minor updates since this is one of the most used rooms in the house.

- Buy the house after you have seen it in person to determine if it is worth the investment and that the description and photographs were honest. Also, take the time to drive to the house. Choosing a location closer to you means you do not have to commute as far while doing the renovations.

- Begin researching the ideal market to decide where people want to live and what the homes are selling for in that area or the 'comps.' This will let you know if there's a house that's listed below market value in a 'hot' neighborhood and how much you could potentially resell it for after updating it. Whatever you estimate that you will need for purchase and renovation, add 20% to the total for incidentals.

- Make an offer on a home with cash. Because there is immense competition in the flipping market, beat the others by going door-to-door and offering the owners cash up front to increase the chances of you owning the home. Be prepared to walk away if the owner is not willing to sell to you at the maximum price you are willing to pay for the property.

- Once you take possession of the house, begin the renovations immediately. Know which projects require contractors and which ones you can do yourself, and don't forget to make a timeline for completion. Also, secure the permits for renovations and display them properly. If you do not, you will risk fines and delays.

- Once your home is ready, list it as soon as possible and begin showing it to buyers. This is why it is wise to have buyers already lined up willing to pay for houses, especially with cash. This will help you resell the house quickly to make a good profit.

Flipping contracts means that you find a seller that is selling their home at a low cost. You make a commitment to purchase and then have your cash buyers lined up to take over the contract. The buyer then pays for the home and takes over the house. You receive payment from the gap between what the buyer pays and what the seller sold it to you for. The process of making money by flipping contracts can be explained in 5 simple steps:

1. Know what the 'right' market looks like. This may not be the market you live in or one that you particularly like. You need to keep an open mind and research the right place. To find this market, look for where other cash buyers are investing. Having the right spot is the most important piece of the puzzle. It will be the difference between making a lot of money and being

stuck with something you cannot get rid of and have to pay.

2. Know the 'right' price. The price is not just how much the house is being sold at but also the price that someone will purchase it from you. To determine if the price is right, consider the following:

    a. Within the block, neighborhood, or market, collect information about all the cash transactions that took place.

    b. Using an online real estate resource, like Realtor.com or Zillow.com, find out what the retail price is estimated at and find the difference.

    c. Determine the average of the differences found. This is considered the 'gap.' The gap represents the average markdown or markup from the retail price for that market's properties.

d. This average gap can be used to determine the approximate price a buyer would pay for a listing that you have found.

e. The listing you found should be lower than the price you would offer to the buyer. You can motivate the seller with an all-cash offer to accept this lower price.

3. Know the types of homes being sold at lower prices. Homes that are about to be repossessed or go on short-sale are excellent options. Houses that are already vacant or are 'distressed' can be viable choices as well. This is not an easy process but using the retail channels can help you find these types of houses. The MLS is

another resource. A third method for finding the right houses is asking around. Talking to the PTO at the local school, other real estate agents or your friends are all great resources. Even if they do not know of anything right away, at least you have put it out there that you are looking for homes to buy and hopefully, they will refer you to something if it comes up.

4. Know who is the 'right' buyer. Once you sign a contract to buy a home, there is typically a 30-day window to close. This means you need to have a few potential buyers available to take that contract within that time frame. These 30-days are considered 'crunch time.' It is a bad time to try to find a buyer. You should have several already ready to take on a contract with cash. This means, before you go under contract on a home, you have identified and contacted potential cash buyers. These are the people you have

found that have paid cash for a house up to 60 days prior. You should send them an introductory note in the mail that explains what you are trying to do. The goal is to establish a relationship with them and find out what they are looking for. This added value helps you when it comes to making the deal.

5. Know who the 'right' seller is. Since you are dealing with sellers that are not necessarily listing their home or are invested in selling their home, this can be harder than it sounds. As you read through a current listing, there are certain words and phrases that can indicate a motivated seller. These phrases can be: "Below market value," "For immediate possession," or "Must sell."

   You can also try to find tax liens on properties, other creditors' liens, or judgments. Again, talking to people around you and around the market you are targeting can reveal potential sellers. Finally, drive around the neighborhoods. Look for homes that look neglected or vacant. If you notice an overgrown lawn, a full mailbox, or broken windows can indicate that the house has been abandoned or is no longer maintained by the current owner.

Chapter 2: Investing in Purchases

Making money in real estate will require an investment to see a profit. One of those types of investments is to buy properties. Some of those purchases include wholesaling houses, bank owned houses or REO's, short-term sales, pre-foreclosures, and land.

Wholesale house investing

The foundation of wholesaling is that you buy a house as-is then turn around and sell it to a buyer who most likely intends to flip it. You are working with another real estate professional rather than a person or business, which is why it is considered wholesale.

To be successful with this strategy, you need to find a seller willing to sell their home in its current state for a low price. Determine if the price is a challenge because it is not usually a straightforward transaction. A buyer will most likely want to spend less than 60% of the anticipated resale value. This means you need to purchase the house for less than that price minus the wholesale fee you want to make. This is your profit so make sure the time and effort are worth that fee. For example, the buyer thinks that they could fix up the house and resell it for $200,000. This means they want to buy it for $120,000. If you want to make $10,000 on the deal, then you have to purchase the house for less than $110,000. If you find a house that fits the parameters, you should do a site visit first and then make an offer.

When you go under contract, bring the contract to a title company that has worked with double closings before to get a receipt. Assign the contract, double close, or simultaneous close with your buyer and collect your wholesale fee.

REOs or Real Estate Owned investing

By REO or real estate owned, we are referring to houses that were returned to the bank after it was foreclosed. Large banks typically have a division dedicated to REO's and work with REO-specific agents. Working with an REO agent can be a challenge because they are dealing with a large volume of houses and small profit margins. This means you should be kind and friendly with an REO agent that you want to work closely with.

When buying an REO you will be expected to place a large deposit down, preferably all cash, and it will be sold as-is. They will also want a quick close. The benefit of an REO is that you are getting a good deal on a house that you can fix and flip, wholesale, etc. for a good profit. To help improve your profit margin, consider using the title company at the bank. The reason is that a foreclosed home has a messy title. This may take time to clean up and that time may cost you extra if you are using an outside title company. If you use the bank, and it goes over the deadline, you will not be charged. Also, since they were the ones who did all the paperwork, they may offer you a title policy at a cheaper rate.

Short-term sales investing

When a seller decides to sell their house at a lower price than what they owe it is called a 'short sale.' This is only possible if the bank or the owner agrees to take a loss on the mortgage. This is sometimes preferable to the lender because they can make more money in a short sale than in an REO. Previously, this purchase would take a long time and requires that the property is under foreclosure. However, there have been some changes that have improved these areas. This type of opportunity is rare and tends to have a lot of competition. Tracking opportunity on sites like redfin.com and foreclosureradar.com and being ready to pay cash can help with this problem. One of the best methods for getting short sales is to work directly with a real estate broker that specializes in short sales because they will probably have inside information about what is available.

Pre-foreclosure investing

The idea of pre-foreclosure investing is almost exactly like purchasing a foreclosed house. The seller is in the process of foreclosing their home, but they still have a few months before it is finalized. These owners have either been over 90 days late on their mortgage payment or *lis pendens* has been filed. This makes these sellers very motivated and willing to deal quickly. They do not want to damage their credit. The lenders also appreciate this sale because it does not require them to foreclose on the property. This process does require a quick deadline, and when a seller is hesitant, confused, or emotional, it can make the process more difficult. In addition, if you miss the deadline, and the property goes into foreclosure, short sale, or goes up for auction, you may face even more competition and more complicated buying requirements.

Land investing

If you are planning to invest in something that does not have as much competition, consider purchasing vacant land. Many real estate professionals avoid land because they believe it will not produce an income and is not as exciting as renovating a house. The wonderful thing about land is that it does not require any additional cost or time. In addition, sellers are more motivated and less emotionally connected to the property. The goal is to purchase the land from these sellers for a very low price and sell it off to developers to build on. This can also be a more long-term investment option. If you recognize that development is trending in the direction of the vacant land, you can purchase it low and wait until it is in demand to sell it for a higher profit. Some people use this a primary investment strategy while others enjoy it as a side business for extra income potential. Either method does have a potential for making a good profit.

These methods of investing in real estate by purchasing property can greatly help you in making money in this field.

Chapter 3: Investing in Rentals

Another form of investing is not just a purchase with the intent to sell but a purchase with the intent to rent. Rentals can be a lucrative option to make consistent income through real estate purchases. Some of the different rental investments include short-term rentals, apartments, commercial leases, vacation property. A final concept that will be introduced in this chapter is lease-to-own. As you will see, and probably gather from the name, this begins as a lease or rental investment with the idea that it will turn into a sale. This could fall into either Chapter 2 or within this chapter, but since it begins as a lease, it is included here.

Short-term rental investing

The rise in Air BNB rentals has made this income opportunity even more attractive. The idea is to purchase a property in a desirable area and offer a short-term rental at a high rent for that time frame. It is even possible to offer several short-term rental agreements at the same time for one property depending on how the house is laid out. Ideally, one or two short-term agreements per month will pay for the monthly mortgage payment, and anything additional is profit you will gain each month. It is important to consider the flow of tourism or visitors in the area if you decide to make use of this method. Some months may be slower than others, which will require you to plan ahead on how to cover the mortgage payment and still make a profit. The inconsistent cash flow is something to consider when thinking about investing in a short-term rental property.

Apartment investing

Apartment investing can be a lucrative option for making steady income every month. The idea is to purchase multiple apartments and rent them out with rental agreements for 1 year or longer. A purchase this large can be an enormous investment, so there are different methods for entering this niche. One of these methods is called 'tenants-in-common.' This involves you and other people going to a building together and splitting the profits. Be aware of the fee structure in the agreement and restrictions or responsibilities expected as a part owner. Another idea is to purchase a smaller building. A third option is to buy a property with multiple units with the intention to live in one unit and rent out the rest. These properties are typically smaller, and the other units can be used to pay the mortgage and provide a profit. The option of renting out the unit you are living will become an available option after a while. You need to live in the property for at least a year before you can use personal home financing.

Commercial lease investing

Commercial leasing can be a variety of properties including retail space, restaurants, industrial spaces, and offices. Profit can be made through both appreciation and income from the property. This is another large initial investment because it has the potential for major monthly and yearly profits. The people leasing the property from you could be anywhere from law firms to a manufacturing company.

Most agreements last for 5 to 10 years or longer, which guarantees an income for an extended period of time. In addition, these properties can be in trendy parts of town or far from desirable living and development areas, depending on the commercial space and tenants. For example, a restaurant will want to be in a more heavily populated area while a distribution company can be further from residential areas. The second method of income from commercial leasing is the appreciation of the property. This is because the value of the commercial property will increase over time.

Of course, the value can decrease but in general, most commercial investments that are made wisely typically result in improved value and appreciation. While demand is the typical method for determining the appreciation of a property, adding value by renovating or improving the property is another method. This method does require investing more money into the property with the intention of getting it back through higher rents, more or better tenants, and increased property value.

Vacation property investing

While it is true that there are no safe locations for vacation rental investments, these can still be a lucrative method for earning a decent amount of profit. Make sure to choose the location carefully. Look for a pleasant house in the best location, so it attracts guests easily, resort or activity-heavy towns are the best for this. These are places like ski towns, Orlando, Hawaii, or even other tourist destinations like Alaska or the Grand Canyon. To determine the income potential, research the competitor's prices in the area and find out what you could realistically charge for renting for a vacation.

Also, consider the rate you would charge for the week to be about 15% higher than your monthly mortgage payment because you will typically have vacancy about 25% of the time. Also, consider additional fees you will need to pay for the property, like association fees or maintenance fees, or the cost for a property manager. Also, having a reliable and good cleaning service that is experienced in working with vacation rentals is important. Make sure to hire people who are dedicated so you can trust them to do their job without much supervision.

Finally, you need to get your property on the market with advertising that allows people to book a schedule online and see what spots are available. In addition, make sure your house is completely stocked. Follow the protocol of other vacation rentals in the area, but the more 'turn-key' it is, the more comfortable your guests will be and the higher the price you could potentially charge. Finally, ask your vacation renters about their experience and keep in touch with them quarterly to encourage them to book again for the following year. A simple newsletter with this message and enticing, fun events happening in the vacation town can be all that is needed to keep the house stocked and the income positive.

Lease-to-own investing

This method of investing is a unique blend of renting and selling. The concept works by you purchasing a house for a low price and then renting the property to a renter who intends to buy the property from you before the lease term ends. You set an expected sale price at the start of the agreement and collect an 'option' fee that is usually about 5%. This fee is a guarantee from you to the renter that you will not sell the property to anyone else while they are in agreement with you and a guarantee from the renter that they intend to buy the property from you at the end of the term or before.

This is an ideal situation for buyers when the market is slow. If you find yourself in a situation where you bought a home to flip, for example, and by the time you have flipped it the market has crashed, and you're at risk of suffering a loss on the property. You could choose to let the property go for less than the amount you invested in it or keep it in anticipation of the market turning around again. The line in the middle of these two options is the lease-to-own. Another reason why you should consider this option is when many sellers are having a hard time purchasing a home in a conventional manner. This is common during a recession. People want to make a purchase, but the difficulty of their financial situation makes expenditures more challenging. Offering this choice to a renter gives them time to gather funds and improve their financial standing, so they are in a better position to purchase the home in the future.

Choosing this investment strategy allows you to buy low, secure a future buyer, and collect monthly mortgage payments for a short time that hopefully makes you some money each month and then sell the property at or above market value. The lease-to-own agreements can be as short as 6 months or longer. Waiting out the time between purchase and sale also allows you to collect on the appreciation of the property for the length of the lease agreement. If you put money into flipping the house, either before or after the renter moved in, you can also set the price to include these costs. Again, this is ideal for situations where you bought low and flipped the house but were not able to resell right away. The challenge is that buyers will be hesitant to commit to a higher price, especially when the market is low and they are in a difficult financial position. Also, if the house is appraised before the sale at a different price than its actual value, the renter may be unwilling or able to purchase the home after all.

This investment is a lower risk strategy than other investments, and it can generate a large profit. Just keep in mind that it is a more of a long-term strategy. While the lease is in existence, you collect the rent and own the property. You also secure a more serious buyer, especially because you have collected the option fee as a guarantee. It is low risk because at the end of the term the tenant will either buy the property of they will not. If they do buy the property as planned, you need to return the option fee in the form of a partial investment in the down payment. You then keep the rent money previously paid and the sale price of the home. If the tenant does not end up purchasing the house, you keep the rent money, the option fee, and the property. You can choose to lease-to-own again or try to sell the home traditionally if the market has improved.

This is not a viable option when money is needed quickly. If you need to lay back the financing, for example, this is probably not the best choice for the property. Again, this is a long game. The return on your initial investment tends to be higher, but it takes longer. Some investors are not willing to wait the time necessary to see that increased profit. This is because the profit can come at the end of the lease when the renter purchases the house or over a long-term rental agreement in the form of monthly rent, it may even come later when you sell the house to another buyer if the first renter does not purchase as expected.

This is also not a great investment strategy for a market for sellers. If you would make a lot of money on a flip right after you complete it, it makes more sense to do that than hold on to it in hopes of making even more down the road. Chances are, if there is a bubble and flips are making a lot, this will not last forever, and you could potentially lose out in the long run.

Chapter 4: Investing in Financial Transactions

There are a few financial transactions that you can also invest in that do not necessarily require you to sell or rent a property. These methods of investing require some financial understanding on your part but also some knowledge on how to turn the opportunity into profit. In this chapter, you will learn about what hard money loans are and how to use them to make a profit. You will learn about real estate tax liens and investment trusts. And finally, you will understand how to maximize on non-performing notes to your financial benefit.

Hard money loans

Some people do not want or cannot get lending for a mortgage in the traditional manner. This is where 'hard money' comes into play. This is money lending that is primarily based on collateral, which is the property. It still requires proof that repayment is feasible, but when money is needed fast, it can be the only option for a buyer. Just as with a traditional loan, credit scores, income, credit history, especially responsible borrowing and consistent repayment are considered. The debt to income ratio is important because it indicates the ability to repay the loan. Unlike a traditional loan, which can be a slower process and has more stringent requirements, hard money is a much better option.

When you are loaned hard money to make a purchase, the most important factor is the collateral. If you are unable to repay the loan, the lender repossesses the collateral and sells it for a profit. This means the collateral needs to be worth it, this piece is more important than the borrower's financial situation.

These loans are intended to be short-term, as it only lasts for up to 5 years. This is good for a borrower because the interest rates are also usually higher. Despite the pitfalls for these types of loans, there are benefits for people who decide to choose this option:

- **Approval is easier**
  This relies heavily on the collateral. Most of the time the lender will only provide what the property is worth and not more for renovations, etc.

- **The process is faster**
  This means the process of getting the money is much faster than a traditional loan. This is mainly thanks to the focus on collateral and less on financial standing. This can be especially advantageous when the market is hot, and the property has multiple offers. Being able to offer a faster financial transaction can mean the success of a purchase over losing a good deal.

- **Agreements can be more flexible**
There is no formal process for underwriting but rather consider each transaction on an individual basis. This opens the door for negotiating things like repayment terms or percentages. These lenders tend to be people and not businesses, which means there is room for customization and discussion.

Low LTV, or loan-to-value, ratios are common in hard money lending. The most you can expect to see is up to 70%. This requires assets from the borrower to qualify for the money. Low LTV ratios create the assurance that, if they do have to take possession of the property, they will be able to sell it quickly and most likely get at least their initial investment back.

Using hard money for fixing and flipping houses is a good example of a situation where it makes sense to use hard money. This is because they only need the money for a short time and have no plans to hold on to the property that long. Once the property is flipped, the borrower would repay the loan as soon as possible, usually within a year. Although some people use a hard money loan to purchase a home to stay in long-term, it is not wise to keep this for long. As soon as you can get a better loan, it is better to refinance.

This method of investing means that you can use this not only to help with fixing and flipping houses when your own financial resources are low, but it can be even more beneficial when you become the lender. Once you have saved up enough profits, you could then begin offering hard money loans to other real estate professionals, making profits from the high-interest rates or from selling an asset if a borrower cannot repay the loan. In this scenario, you now become the investor.

You can market yourself to your community, or the market you think would benefit the most from this offer and develop a relationship with borrowers to begin lending and generating passive income quickly. You can do this individually or partner with other real estate professionals to offer hard money loans as well.

Real estate tax liens

This is an investment opportunity that is frequently overlooked by other real estate professionals. A tax lien is when the city or county where the property is situated puts a lien on it when the owner does not pay taxes on it. An unpaid amount owed by the owner receives a legal claim by the county. This lien restricts the buyer from selling or refinancing until the taxes are paid. This will then start the process of removing the lien. When there is a lien on a property, some lenders will then choose to sell the property at an auction. The buyer at the auction can negotiate to lower an interest rate or offer a higher bid to secure a prime property.

When bidding on a tax lien contract, it is important to be aware of repairs you might have to make and to prepare for unexpected costs. Eviction is another cost and hassle to prepare for. Another thing you should be aware of is the value of a property that may be lower than the lien. To determine if the property can provide a profit, take the tax lien amount and divide it by the current value of the property. If the percentage is higher than 4%, it is not worth the effort. Also, find out if there are other liens on the property. This could prevent you from taking control of the house.

To purchase a tax lien, it is required that the lien is immediately repaid to the county or city. Then the owner repays you as the investor plus interest. The interest rate can vary from as low as 5% and as high as 35%. The owner can be given anywhere from 6 months to 3 years. In the rare instance that the owner cannot repay you as an investor, you can foreclose on the property to recover the investment.

Real estate investment trusts

These trusts, nicknamed REITs, are traded on the stock exchange, and any professional can buy shares of them. It is advisable, since these are like public stock, that you work with a financial planner, broker, or investor to choose the best options for you. As with other trading options, the value fluctuates throughout the day, and their net income is used to measure to measure their performance. There is no need to have the tax document, Schedule K-1, to invest in REITs.

Non-performing notes

This is similar to a tax lien, but the property owner has stopped making payments to the lender. Prior to placing a property in foreclosure, you can purchase the loans that are behind in payments, usually for a significant discount. These are not listed through the MLS, meaning you can get inventory that is new and inexpensive. Once you take control of the note, you can decide to do a variety of things with it like selling it to another investor, fix and flip it, or rent it out.

One method for making money without much investment or time is to modify the loan and assist the current homeowner to refinance. This means that if you purchase a note for $100,000 but the home is worth $200,000, and the current owners are 'upside down' paying on a loan of $250,000, you can adjust the loan balance to $200,000 at a 5% interest rate and set the monthly mortgage payment to an affordable amount for the homeowner. Once the homeowner can make at least 3 months of on-time payments, you can refinance the loan, paying off the note, doubling your money, and helping a homeowner! Another method is to hold on to the note, so the homeowner continues paying you and once it becomes a performing note, you can resell it to another investor for more than the amount that you paid.

Other options to make money on non-performing notes include selling them through a short sale or foreclosing on the property. A short sale is good for the delinquent homeowners that want out of the house, and there are no other liens on the property. It is possible to do a short sale with other liens on the property, but it becomes more difficult. Foreclosure should be the last option considered for making a profit because it yields the lowest return. This option should be used only in the worst-case scenario where the potential return on the initial investment is less than acceptable.

Chapter 5: Representing

There are a few additional methods for making money through real estate that is not about purchasing a home or investing a lot of money to see a return. Some of those methods include diversifying who you represent. For example, you could represent homeowners and sellers, commercial clients, and even other investors.

To understand how to make money as an agent for buyers and sellers, it is important to understand how each and every one gets paid in the process. It all begins with the seller who pays the broker for the listing. When the listing broker obtains the money, they then pay out to the agent responsible for the listing and the broker representing the buyer. When the buyer's broker receives the money, they pay out the agent responsible for the buyer.

Represent homebuyers

To be a buyer's agent, you are required to work with a broker. You cannot be paid directly from the buyer, so the money first goes to the brokers, both the listing and the buying brokers, and then to you as the agent. Occasionally, you could be paid a salary through your brokerage firm. However, most of the time you are considered a contractor working for commission.

This commission can be up to 3% of the sale price of the house the buyer selects, and this can differ based on local market habits and what the seller desires. This is a percentage the seller determines when they list a property so you can go into a house knowing a rough estimate of what you would make. It is important to understand that some brokers will take a portion of the commission of the buyer's agent, sometimes as much as 50%. The broker you're working with will determine how this would be. It is something you should consider before deciding to work with them.

Represent home sellers

As mentioned previously in this chapter, the seller's broker pays a selling agent after the sale. This means that you get one of the largest commissions paid out as a seller's agent. This commission can be up to 6% of the property's sale price. Representing a homeowner in the process of selling their house can also carry the title, 'listing agent.' Homeowners will expect you to help prepare their property for the sale, market it to potential buyers and other agents, show it, and help throughout the process of the sale. Another valuable tool to provide to the seller is an approximate value or price for the house. It is in your best interest to try and get the most for that person's house, but it needs to be a realistic price based on the current market, other prices in the neighborhood, and condition of the house among other considerations.

When listing a house for a seller, remember that commission percentages can be flexible, so be prepared to negotiate, especially if it is a property that you expect a good return on, even with a lower commission percentage. Finally, remember that the percentage paid in commission is also split with the buyer's brokerage and the seller's brokerage. Sometimes this can be as much as a 50/50 split. Take this into consideration when representing a property and negotiating a commission percentage.

Representing commercial clients

To represent a commercial client, a special real estate license designation is required in many states. In certain situations, you could choose to work for a landlord and try to find a business to lease available space in the building. In this situation, when a lease is signed, you could receive commission up to 3% of the total amount of rent to be paid over the lease's lifespan. This method is one of the most traditional methods of commercial representation. This benefits both the landlord and you when you get the highest rent possible for space.

On the other hand, you could work with tenants looking for space. This relationship is different because you can scout multiple properties and negotiate the lowest rent possible for that client. Negotiating and deciphering the lease terms for the client are two major benefits the business will receive from you in this scenario. Because you are bringing a business to a space instead of hunting for a tenant, you will receive a portion of the commission the broker working with the landlord will receive when the lease is signed.

Occasionally, you can be successful representing both landlords and tenants. However, this situation can become conflicted when you show a property to the client that you also represent. It is important to remember that you are responsible for finding the tenant the best space for their needs, regardless of who is listing it. The conflict of interest arises when the landlord is looking for an immediate tenant, which you are also responsible for finding, but the tenant is not a good fit for that space. This can become a 'grey area,' but it can be quite lucrative when done ethically and wisely.

Representing other real estate investors

Working with an investor is very different than working for a commercial or residential client. There is typically a lot less emotion built into the sale, and they are looking solely for opportunities to make money rather than a property they will be in for a long time. This means the conversations and deals will be different. Also, most residential or commercial clients are looking for a single property while investors will be most comfortable taking on multiple deals. They will also be more frequent customers since they buy and sell frequently. In addition, investors tend to already know how the process works so there are a lot less 'surprises' or 'tough conversations' about how it all works. And finally, they can offer their own advice on how you can invest well in real estate and other investors you could work with.

There are several types of investors, like flippers, wholesalers, and those who buy a property to hold on to for a determined amount of time, probably for a rental property. To successfully work with any kind of investor, you should focus both on clear communication and speed. Encouraging them to be realistic about their goals and methods can help you get them an investment faster, which means money in both your pockets.

Chapter 6: Developing

Making money in real estate does not mean you cannot have a hand in creating the opportunity out there in the form of leads for realtors and the actual properties. Some real estate professionals enjoy the development side of the business, creating the needs they identify in a market to generate their own cash flow. Some of the development opportunities that you can consider include generating leads, helping realtors with leads, developing rental properties, and the establishment of granny flats, also called mother-in-law living quarters. Other times the property already exists but you can repurpose it into another function, like converting houses into multifamily units.

Redeveloping multifamily units

When you take over an already existing property, whether it is already laid out to be a multifamily unit or you plan on making it that way, you open the door for redevelopment with immense income potential. The property can be sold for a profit because it will generate a lot of money for another investor, or you can hold onto it and reap the continual benefits of monthly income and yearly property appreciation. Before you redevelop a multifamily unit, consider the rental market in the area. Determine what tenants are paying in the area and determine if the cost of what you would charge per month to make a profit would fall within the current range.

It is important to note other rental properties in the area and their vacancy rates. If there is an overabundance of open apartments, owners will be more willing to take on questionable tenants and possibly lower their rates, making your new development more of a challenge to fill in that area.

When you select a property, make sure it can be rented as a multifamily unit, especially if it was not made for that purpose. There are typically laws governing where these units can be, so be aware of what the restrictions are in your area and determine if it's worth going through that process for that property and whether redeveloping it is feasible. This can be a lucrative option, especially if the property is unique to that area. Some areas lack rental and apartment options, while other multifamily units can offer a unique living environment that is attractive to that area. If you can develop these kinds of properties, you can get a high return in either the direct sale of the property or the rental of the space from month to month.

Leads for realtors

Leads are the life source of real estate agents. The number one concern, focus, and cause for anxiety is generating enough leads to make a decent living. Without properties to sell or people to sell them to, there is no money to be made. Having a website, marketing for leads, and networking to develop contacts takes time and requires up-to-date knowledge, much of which real estate professionals do not have time or interest in. To make money generating leads for other real estate professionals, it is important that you dedicate time to doing just those tactics. One of the most beneficial and time-friendly methods of generating leads is to create a website that potential buyers are attracted to. Besides making it look attractive, it needs to contain interesting content that drives people to view the site and fill out a lead form, indicating an interest in purchasing or listing a property. Providing content about real estate in the area and also other interesting information about the market can be helpful for getting people to take a step further and fill out a form to stay 'in the loop' with all your interesting content.

Once you begin generating leads from your website you can do some things to make money. One of the most obvious and most financially beneficial is to sell the leads to realtors looking for more opportunities. Another method is to sell advertising space on the website. This could be sold to other real estate professionals who want to get the leads for themselves or for businesses that would benefit from this type of traffic. Finally, having an 'expert' contribute to the content of the site can be another option, but it is better to do this once the site is well-known and respected for lead generation and quality information. When a professional wants to get their name associated with your website you can charge them a fee for getting space on the site.

Another way you can make money with a website that generates leads is to make a network that requires a fee to access. For example, you may create a universal homepage that contains your interesting content, but then you create a subpage for a paying realtor that they can use to provide their own content to potential buyers and sellers or generate their own leads. The benefit of them connecting with you is getting access to a professional and well-maintained website with online marketing that benefits them as well as all the other realtors networking through your site. In addition, the leads they generate go directly to them, but they can also pay more per month to get general leads that are developed through the homepage.

Using the online method for networking is the easiest, most cost-effective, and most timesaving method. Generating leads by doing more traditional campaigns can work, but they require a bit more of a time and financial investment. Creating a quality webpage with decent traffic can give you a steady stream of income in a variety of ways.

Help realtors connect with leads

Sometimes it is not about getting leads, but it is about connecting with them. It may be that the realtor is not sure how to go about soliciting by phone or email, or they do not want to put in the time trying to convert their leads. This is where an intermediary can be beneficial. If you take on the process of 'setting appointments' for realtors, they can rest a little easier knowing that you have done a lot of the hard work for them. You then can charge a fee per appointment set or a flat hourly fee for how many hours per week you call and set appointments for them. It may seem like a waste of money to hire someone to connect with the leads, especially since they are so valuable, but the reality is that not all leads are created equal. A list that is bought through a website, like described above, will have a lower conversion rate than a referral from a previous client. This means that a real estate professional may have to call 100 website leads or email 1,000 leads before setting 1 appointment. To save time, they hire someone else to make those phone calls and emails so they can focus on the people in front of them or other marketing strategies to make money.

Developing rental properties

While this concept has been introduced earlier as a form of an investment, actually building the property to be sold is another way to make money. In this money making venture, you buy the land, develop the property, but also manage the rental as a landlord. You have full control over all the aspects of the property and reap the rewards on a monthly basis, including the yearly appreciation of the property. If you are a person that likes to do things by yourself and are handy with construction and development tasks, this can be an even more lucrative option. This trait will not only serve you well in the development of the property but when you become a landlord as well. The benefit of renting a property is that often the landlord is responsible for things like yard work and repairs. If you can do these yourself without hiring a contractor, you can save a lot of money.

If you need to call in contractors to help, pick those you have worked with before that are reliable, do quality work, and give you a good deal on their services. This is also helpful in the process of finding people to rent your space. Having real estate connections that specialize in working with tenants can be helpful in making sure you are fully rented out and making a profit right away. Knowing people that are familiar with rentals and working with them is important because once you have a tenant, it becomes a 24-hour role. Having people who you can call to assist with needed repairs or assistance can make a big difference in keeping units rented and tenants happy.

Developing granny flats or mother-in-law living quarters or accessory dwellings

There has been a rise in the need and interest in 'granny flats' throughout the country. These are also called mother-in-law suites or accessory dwellings. In fact, there are a variety of names given to these smaller houses that are built on another property's lot. Adding this type of structure to an already existing house boosts the value of the house and can also increase a homeowner's income if they choose to rent it out. Teaming with a development team to create these tiny houses can be beneficial, or you could build several on a single lot of land you purchased and collect the rent yourself. Either way, developing these granny flats can give you a nice source of income, and you have a unique feature to offer to the market.

Chapter 7: Diversifying

Diversifying what you do to make money is a smart way to guarantee your success. This means that your income is not dependent on one stream. For example, if all you do is fix and flip houses, if the market crashes so does all your money. But if you mix and match different options, you can enjoy a more steady and reliable stream of income. Some additional ways that you can diversify your skill set include becoming a broker, property manager, appraiser, home inspector, or agent for corporate housing.

Becoming a broker

When you diversify and become a broker, there are a few important questions to ask yourself. Ideally, this process will not cost you a lot of money, so it is advisable that you try to be a broker who does not require an office. To determine if an office space is necessary, consider the following:

- What kind of clients do you want to work with? If you represent mainly buyers as a broker, you probably do not need an office space. If you are a seller's broker, you are more likely expected to have an office space. For example, a seller will meet a listing broker where they will work with their selling agent and ultimately the money is exchanged for the sale. Most of the time the buyer, the buyer's agent, and the buyer's broker will meet at the selling broker's office to conclude the sale and paperwork. Part of this is a mental game for the seller, but part is a convenience for the sale.

- Is mobility an option for you? This means you need to access information on the fly, so having a laptop, wireless and mobile printer, and a portable scanner is important. This may require you to make an investment at the beginning to gain these necessary tools.

- Do your clients want you to have a professional meeting space? Even if you can work on the go, some types of clients might want to meet in a professional space. This goes for realtors that will be contracting under you as well. They expect a broker to provide support and professionalism. Sometimes having a computer and internet access that they can use when meeting with clients is all they need for the sale.

- Do you have the ability to get a digital signature? Digital signatures are now more acceptable, so it is important you have the ability for your clients to sign the various real estate documents with a stylus on a screen. If you already have a portable printer and scanner, this is not completely necessary, but it can save you a lot of time and resources over the long haul. Regardless of the method of signature, you still need a printer to provide copies to your clients after everything has been signed.

It is becoming more and more acceptable to work outside of an office, especially since sellers and buyers are becoming more comfortable with technology and its benefits. However, there probably will always be a demand for a professional space for meeting clients. This can be especially true for sellers, investors, and larger purchases.

Becoming a property manager

Establishing a successful career in real estate can take time, and when you are just starting out, it is a good idea to find ways to earn an income as you build your business. This is where property management comes into play. Property managers are typically paid a salary for their role, which can help provide a base while commissions are low and far between. This may not be the most lucrative method for making money, but it is good to diversify so you have a source of steady income.

The role of a property manager is multi-faceted. It requires tenant screening, the rental of the house, collecting rent, handling repair requests, some accounting, and other customer service and office duties. You can choose to work for an established property management company, or you can try to manage properties on your own. If you decide to work for a company, the pay will most likely be lower but stable, while working on your own means you have the potential to yield a higher profit but it's not as reliable.

As a property manager, you can expect to earn anywhere from 5 to 10 percent of the rent on the managed properties. It is also possible to charge a leasing fee, which is typically equivalent to a month's worth of rent. This means that to make a large amount of money as a property manager, you need to manage multiple properties. Another added benefit of becoming a property manager is that you can create a contract with the landlord that requires them to list the property with you if they plan on selling it. This means you will make money on the rental of the unit and on the sale if they decide to offload the property. It can also give you access to a property before any other real estate professional, which is a prime asset to have!

This money making opportunity may not be a full-time career, but it can provide enough money and time to focus on ramping up other sides of your business.

Becoming an appraiser

Some real estate professionals join the industry for this one avenue because it can be a rewarding experience. Typically this is a field position, requiring you to visit various properties throughout the day, working from a home-based office. This means you are not tied to a desk all day, but you're not on the road all the time either. Your income is not affected if a loan does not close. You are a contractor and paid a flat fee for your services. While all this may sound lucrative, it is not easy to establish yourself as an appraiser in your market and may require you to 'pay your dues' to your real estate market before you can become successful in this area.

Some of the things to consider when becoming an appraiser includes:

- **Find a mentor**
  This can be quite a challenge because an appraiser might not want to share the workload by training you to be their competition. Make sure you find someone who does great work and is compliant. Also, make sure they are not taking advantage of you or are cheating you so you won't get the information you need to know. Looking to family and friends in this line of work can be an advantage.

- **Certified appraisers are highly sought after**
  This means that once you do get licensed, you also want to get certified. It is possible to become certified without becoming licensed, but that process is typically longer to achieve. The benefit to taking this extra step is the limited competition, higher demand, and the opportunity to gain a large income. You can charge more for your services, especially if you are both licensed and certified.

- **Speaking of fees, these will vary from place to place**
  Usually, smaller cities pay appraisers more than those that work in larger markets. This is because of competition. Smaller markets have fewer appraisers, especially licensed and certified appraisers. Larger cities will have more competition, which necessitates that you lower your fees just to compete. A small-

market appraiser could expect a fee of $100 up to $500.

Becoming a home inspector

A home inspection can be a difficult profession to take and does require some expertise, but it is possible to make a good amount of money diversifying your sources of income by becoming a home inspector.

If you have experience in the construction industry, you will have a leg-up in this profession. It is not necessary, however, and professionalism is more important now than in the past. While it does not cost much to start a home inspection business, some people would rather choose a well-established home inspector or to purchase a franchise. A franchise can be a good start if you are new to the industry. You will get the benefit of their reputation, training, and marketing but will have to pay fees and costs more to start.

This line of work involves you performing a visual inspection of the property that someone owns or is planning to buy. This is a full inspection that goes from the top of the roof to the bottom of the visible foundation and everything in between. You also need to test and check internal systems like HVAC, electrical, and plumbing. The land is also inspected for proper grading and drainage. The purpose of the inspection is to say if it is working correctly or if it's in need of repair in some area. You must indicate if there is something that is not working which might negatively impact the value of the house or is hazardous to people. You do not 'pass' or 'fail' a property, but you do report what you find.

Becoming a corporate housing provider or agent

Being a corporate housing agent means that you help businesses find an apartment or living arrangement, typically fully-furnished, for employees. All utilities and services are also included in the cost of the rental. These are popular for businesses that have employees that travel to various locations often or are only there for a short time but need something longer than a hotel stay. To make a profit, you could offer a property as a corporate housing option or find existing corporate housing options and work with businesses to fill the spaces. You could work as an independent contractor for the business or for the corporate housing property. Each option pays a percentage of commission for fulfilling a short-term lease.

Chapter 8: Bonus Money Making Ideas

In addition to all the described methods for making money with real estate, there are some other ideas out there that are harder to classify. These are labeled here as 'bonus' ideas that can potentially turn a profit for you. Some of these ideas include crowdfunding, house hacking, and syndicates, among others. If you have not already started gathering ideas of how you can diversify your income through various real estate endeavors, maybe you will find some interesting options here.

1031 exchange

The concept of a 1031 exchange is actually quite simple. It is a way to defer your taxes. It is not avoiding taxes, but a mere deference. This can be very beneficial if used wisely. Used well, you will not only save on taxes, but you will gain substantial wealth. When you sell a property, you are expected to pay taxes on the gain. Utilizing the 1031 exchange, you are allowed to 'defer' property tax payments on a sale when you can show you are using the profit to purchase another similar investment, like property.

This does not have to apply only to real estate, but that is where it is seen the most often. There are rules that the IRS developed for a 1031 exchange, and they are relatively strict. The IRS is fine with you reinvesting the money that would have been taxed because they are hoping you will make even more on the next deal and eventually they will get a larger sum. The taxes will have to be paid at some point after all. But in the meantime, taxes are not paid out, and you can reinvest the profits from a previous investment into other avenues, as long as they are similar in nature. This means you need to stay in the real estate market with the funds, and you do not need to stay within the same type of real estate. You could move from rental properties to flipping houses or commercial endeavors without incurring the taxes each switch would face when you sold and purchased another.

Crowdfunding for real estate

There are now online platforms for investors to get together and pool their resources to invest in various projects. There are typically two types of investments in crowdfunding: debt, such as a mortgage loan that is repaid and the interest on the loan is split between the investors, or equity, such as property for a stake in the equity or part of rental payments.

Should you choose to invest in a crowdfunding investment, you can expect an investment that is more transparent than other investment options. For example, REITs may not disclose everything about a property, making it riskier while crowdfunding lays all the details on the table. In addition, crowdfunding is more accessible. You do not need to have large sums of cash to invest and make a profit. There are also more investment opportunities for a variety of types of products that are all listed in one place. There are also tax breaks that are possible when using crowdfunding because you are investing in an income property.

If you decide to try out crowdfunding, make sure you research things first and pick the best platform for what you want to do. Also, before making an investment of this nature, talk with a financial advisor to make sure there are no issues or loopholes in the agreements. It is also important to make sure you recognize how long the agreement is for. Some investments have long timelines, this can tie up your cash that you could be using for other deals.

House hacking and free-living

The term 'house hacking' refers to a property that you purchase as an investment that you will also live in. You can live in a house while flipping it, or you can purchase a multifamily property and live in a unit while the other units are rented to tenants. Ideally, this process would allow you to live in the property for free while the tenant pays the mortgage payment, and then some. This investment strategy is particularly advantageous for new real estate professionals. This method of money making also provides hands-on learning and easy property management because your investment is right next to your tenants.

To be successful financially in this strategy, you need to consider the actual cash flow and profit as well as the saved expenses. When you do not have to pay the mortgage or any expenses on the property, and you do not need to pay for your living arrangements, you are saving a substantial amount of money per month. Then add in the amount of profit you get from rent each month, and you are now making a decent amount of money. It is a wise idea to invest not with only the house hacking model in mind but also what you plan to do when you decide to move out. It needs to make sense as an investment when you decide to leave. You could decide to rent out the extra unit or sell it completely. If you rent it out, consider not just the increase in rent revenue but also the increase in expenses and vacancy risk. You still need to come out ahead each month.

Syndicate properties

Another method of investing where you pool funds with another investor or group of investors is called real estate syndication. The funds can then purchase a property or be used to contribute to the purchase of a larger project with other real estate syndicates. Investing in this nature is the most advantageous for commercial properties or larger multifamily units, such as apartment buildings.

There are three main methods for profiting from real estate syndicates:

1. The syndicate you are part of will be responsible for creating a deal, researches the viability of the investment and discovers the property. For all this work the syndicate will receive acquisition fees.

These can be as high as 5% of the cost of acquisition or can be paid out in a single payment. If you did the majority of the work and then brought on other investors, you can take a larger percentage of the fee. However, be sure that you won't end up taking too much and risk losing the investors for later projects.

2. If you're the one managing the relationship between the investors in the syndicate and property that is purchased you can collect an 'asset management' fee. This is typically 1% of the revenue grossed from the profits each month. If you are managing the property or are working with the property manager, you are still required to spend time and effort on making sure the investment is thriving while keeping in communication with the rest of the group as well as ensuring their pay is distributed on time. This is your payment for all that work.

3. Appreciation and a split of the cash flow are the final methods of payment. For example, if you decide not to be the investor that finds and manages the property but simply puts money into the pool, this is what you would get in return. If a property performs as expected throughout the year, the profits of the investment will be split between you and the other investors and the appreciation of the property is available to you as a partial owner.

Creating an effective website

Previously in this book, we discussed hosting a website to generate leads, but that is not the only type of website that will make you a successful real estate professional. Creating an effective website that outlines and showcases who you are and what you do can generate leads, solidify sellers and buyers, and open other doors for financial gain. This may not be a direct method for generating revenue, but it can be quite advantageous if you learn how to use it properly.

The basic elements you need on your website to make it effective are:

- **Your name and your real estate logo**
  Make sure people know exactly who they are looking at and what you represent. To help your viewer remember this information, place these details in the upper left-hand side.

- **Tell people what you want them to do**
  This may seem presumptive, but it is a call to action that makes sure people do not misinterpret what you do or are looking for. This can be a tagline like: 'Sell your house today. Click here,' or 'Find your next home here.' Place this message across from your name and logo, in the upper right-hand corner.

- **Keep the layout simple and easy to navigate**
  You want your visitors to find the information they are searching for easily, but you also want to direct them to the information you want them to see. This can require an intuitive graphic design, but that doesn't make it any less important. Remember, the goal is to convert these visitors to clients so each page should have this goal.

- **Promote dominant and bold headlines**
  This is what will catch your visitor's eye first. Do not worry about being clever or cute. Keep it clear and direct.

- **Choose graphics wisely**
  A well-chosen graphic that aligns with your message is important. Do not choose

a 'pretty' image or something very generic. Make this image count.

- **Choose color carefully**
  Use strategic placements of bold colors that drive the visitor's eye to specific places on the webpage. This will ensure they will see the messages that you want them to see.

- **Include a sub-header that leads into the text of the page**
  Make sure the important messages are held in the header and sub-header with supporting details in the text. People do not spend a lot of time reading web pages and using this strategy will make sure they get your message.

- **The text or message you presented needs to benefit the visitor**
  If you want to promote a feature you offer, make sure it stresses how it will help a potential client.

- **Make sure you offer the visitor something for considering you and spending time on your site**
  If you want them to enter contact information, give them something in return, such as a free eBook or any other useful item.

- **You must have a place to collect a visitor's information**
  This form can be on the main page or on a separate 'Contact' page. Wherever it is located on the website, make sure each page can link to it.

- **Do not label links and buttons generically**
  Customize the links with messages like 'Give me my free eBook!' Also, make sure each link and button actually works.

- **Remain professional and show visitors you are a business**
  Tabs like, 'About us,' and 'Office location' and 'Contact information' are good ways to create trust in your professionalism.

- **Put keywords into the background of your website**
  Doing this optimizes the website for better search results. Some website generators offer the ability to do this, but it may be worth investing in a professional to optimize your site.

- **Direct your visitor where you want to go by placing most of the content** and direction on the left side of the pages

- **Always check your website and constantly tweak to improve its efficiency**

Conclusion

Thank you for making it through to the end of *Real Estate Management*, let's hope it was informative and that it provided you with all of the tools you need to achieve your goals whatever they may be.

The next step is to choose some of the different methods that interested you within this book and do further research on the concept. Be confident in how you will invest your time and money in a real estate venture and then begin! Begin working for yourself, begin making real money, begin diversifying your income streams, and begin living the life you have envisioned! There are so many options available to you so you can earn a decent amount of money in this industry. Explore a few and keep with the ones that work. If something is not performing the way you want it to, modify the approach or try a different method we outlined here in the book.

Hopefully, you have found the information in this book informative and applicable to your goals as a real estate professional. Take calculated risks and enjoy the returns on your real estate savvy. Your decisions will determine whether or not you will be successful in real estate, which hopefully was obvious as you read this book. Take those tools and apply them to your business and watch your bank account swell!

Finally, if you found this book useful in any way, a review on Amazon is always appreciated!

Description

Entering the world of real estate can be exciting, but it can also be daunting. There are so many new concepts and methods for making money that it can be overwhelming. And even when you get going and start gaining ground, there are still so many other ways that you can earn even more, sometimes with hardly any additional time or money involved. Part of what drew you to the real estate industry in the first place is the income potential and the freedom of working (basically) for yourself. It is a way to get paid for the time and effort you put in while you constantly get to change and move to different locations on a daily basis if you want.

Choosing just one niche or client type can be a successful venture for some real estate professionals, but diversifying your income sources can open more doors and ensure you are always bringing in a profit, even if one market is slow. Explore some of the common and uncommon real estate choices explained throughout this book and decide which ones would fit with your personality and goals. Some people may be in this for a part-time venture while others want to be 'moguls.' Using this book as a guide, you can find what will work for you and go after it!

The purpose of this book is to provide the tools and resources to reach those goals through real estate ventures. Some of the concepts require you to take a greater risk for the chance at getting a larger reward while others are low risk but provide a steady income. You can choose to invest in real estate solo, partner with other real estate professionals, or even get additional training and licensure to serve more clients and markets. Whatever your goal, whatever your experience, this book will give you sound advice with details on how to successfully make a profit in this line of work.

This book highlights the following topics:

- An introduction on how to fix and flip houses for profit

- A comprehensive outline of over 10 investment strategies that can return small to large returns on your investment

- Discussion on how to flip contracts for profit without even having to invest any money or much time

- Learn how to make money on renting property

- Discover the application and benefit of doing lease-to-own

- Explore the various financial strategies you can use to make money, even while helping current homeowners along the way

- Choose or expand the clients you represent by viewing the options outlined in this book, such as homeowners, home buyers, commercial clients, and other retail investors

- Consider if developing is an income option for your success

- Generate resources for other real estate professionals to help them succeed as well as you

- Determine how to become more than 'just' a real estate agent

- Look beyond the traditional sources and open your mind to amazing other income generators like:

    o 1031 exchange

- Househacking
- Crowdfunding
- Syndication

And much, much more!

www.ingramcontent.com/pod-product-compliance
Lightning Source LLC
Chambersburg PA
CBHW052332220526
45472CB00001B/393